Factual Advisers
Dr. Angela V. John
Thames Polytechnic, London

Toshi Marks
Centre for the Study of Contemporary Japan
Essex University

Series and Book Editor: Nicole Lagneau
Teacher Panel: Hilary Bourdillon, Jo Donovan
Designer: Ewing Paddock
Production: Rosemary Bishop
Picture Research: Diana Morris

A MACDONALD BOOK

© Macdonald & Company (Publishers) Ltd 1987

First published in Great Britain in 1987 by Macdonald
& Company (Publishers) Ltd, London & Sydney
A BPCC plc company
All rights reserved

Printed and bound by Henri Proost
Turnhout, Belgium

Macdonald & Co (Publishers) Ltd
Greater London House
Hampstead Road
London NW1 7QX

British Library Cataloguing in Publication Data
Sproule, Anna
    Solidarity. — (Women history makers).
    1. Women social reformers — Juvenile
    literature
    I. Title   II. Series
    303.4'84   HN49.W6
    ISBN 0-356-13120-3
    ISBN 0-356-13121-1 Pbk

Acknowledgements
We would like to thank The Society
of Authors on behalf of the Bernard
Shaw Estate for permission to
quote from *Dr Annie Besant: 50
Years in Public Work*, 1924, by
Bernard Shaw. Also to Stanford
University Press for permission to
quote sections from *Flowers in
Salt, The Beginnings of Feminist
Consciousness in Modern Japan*,
by Professor Sharon L. Sievers
(pages 49, 51, 112, 127, 128,
134, 195, 218, 226); to Columbia
University Press for permission to
quote from *The Industrial Workers
of the World* by Paul Brissenden.

We have made every effort to trace
the owners of copyright material
and acknowledge the source of
quotes from the following:
Mother Jones — The Miners' Angel,
by Dale Fetherling, Southern
University Press, 1974.
*Peasants, Rebels and Outcastes: the
Underside of Modern Japan*, Mikiso
Hane, Pantheon Books, New York,
1982.
Associated University Presses,
London and Toronto, 1984, *Fukuda
Hideko and the Woman's World of
Meiji Japan* by Sharlie C. Ushioda
from *Japan in transition* (ed. Hilary
Conroy and others).

Illustrations:
Paul Cooper 24, 37

Photographs
Archives of Labor & Urban Affairs,
Wayne State University: cover, front
left, 6—7 (Davie King Collection),
34r, 35, 40.
BBC Hulton Picture Library: cover,
front right, 19.
BPCC: 25, 39, 40.
Bridgeman Art Library: 12 (City of
Manchester Art Galleries).
Carnegie Library, Pittsburgh:
32—33, 32l.
Colorado Historical Society: 36.
Mary Evans Picture Library: 17t, 21.
International Society for
Educational Information, Tokyo: 9l,
22, 28.
Keystone-Mast Collection: cover,
foreground, 23b.
Library of Congress: 33.
London University, SOAS: back
cover, 30, 31.
Mansell Collection: 10, 11, 14, 26.
National Museum of Labour
History: 5, 8, 13, 16t, 18, 43.
Popperfoto: 23t, 27.
Ann Ronan Picture Library: 15b,
17b, 20.
T.U.C. Library: 15t.
UPI/Bettmann Newsphotos: 9r, 38t,
41.

SOLIDARITY

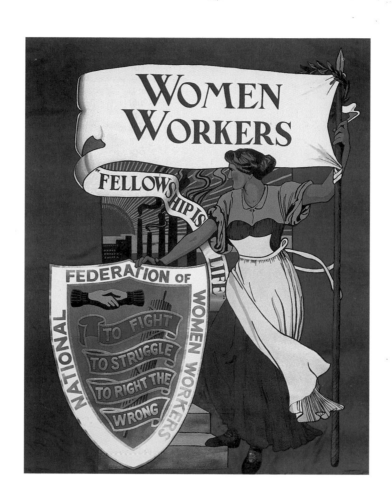

Anna Sproule

Macdonald

About this book

Half the people in the world are women. So why do women appear so seldom in books on history? One reason is that until recently, history has been mainly about public events; many people thought that women should not take part in these. But, all the same, some women defied what people thought. Their public achievements made history, or would have done if historians had remembered to take notice of them.

For the past hundred years, many male historians have shared the 19th century view that a woman's real place was at home, serving her family. If they found proof to the contrary, they often didn't recognize it, or ignored it. (The only people they could never ignore were rulers.) Often, they summed up women's achievements in a couple of sentences, or a footnote in small print.

The books in this series aim to put the women history-makers back where they belong: in the world they helped change, and in the way that we remember that world.

The three women you will read about here belonged to the world of the late 19th century and early 20th centuries, but they lived in different countries. One, called Annie Besant, was British; another, Kageyama Hideko, was Japanese. The third was an Irish immigrant to the United States of America; her full name was Mary Harris Jones but she was known across America as 'Mother Jones'. This book shows what they had in common.

How to use this book
When studying the past, all historians try to go back to what the people of the past actually wrote and said. In the sections of this book marked **'Witness'**, you can read some of the things said by people living at the time of Annie Besant, Hideko and Mary Harris Jones, and comments from the women themselves. Keep a look out for these, and look out, too, for the sections marked **'Action'**. These will raise questions about how history was written in the past. They ask you to test the reliability of sources and to find out what has motivated people in the past.

Linked together in a common aim: in the United States of America, men, women and children join together on May Day, 1917, in remembering people who died for the workers' cause. The newspaper recalls the name of the trade union involved: the Industrial Workers of the World, often called the 'Wobblies'.

Contents

Women and history

'Solidarity' is a new word in most people's ordinary speech. Yet, it is not a new idea. It means sympathy, loyalty, banding or working together, and it remains one of the important forces that keep societies from falling apart. Usually, the people who band together into a 'solid' group are doing it in support of something; almost always, they are doing it in defiance of something else.

Britain, Japan and the United States are three great industrial powers and the three women in this book lived and worked in an industrial setting. Two of them, Annie Besant and Mary Harris Jones, were strongly involved in trade union work, while Japan's Kageyama Hideko tried to improve the lives of her country's industrial workers by freeing them from social oppression. But the guiding union principle of 'United we stand' can be applied to the efforts of all three women in their demands for social justice.

Annie Besant's Britain was even more strongly divided by class differences than it is today. Annie herself led middle-class thinkers into helping the workers. In the 1880s, the working class's struggle to win political power and free itself from appalling poverty was an example of solidarity. In Japan at the same period, women formed a huge, oppressed under-class of their own. According to one of the first feminists, Hideko, their salvation lay in female solidarity. 'Rise up', she told them, 'and build your own women's movement.' In the face of still further oppression, some took her advice and finally succeeded in bringing about reforms.

Today, the idea of solidarity has a strong industrial flavour. We are familiar with the struggle of the members of 'Solidarity', Poland's famous independent trade union banned in 1981. Polish workers banded together both in their demands for big political reforms and in their defiance of the government. But in this book, only one of the three women, Mary H. Jones, was exclusively concerned with workers' solidarity. Annie Besant was concerned with solidarity with the low-paid and Hideko with solidarity with other women. All three women found they faced problems that were often similar. Sometimes, they even provided the same solutions. This book shows how they reached their solutions and how far they worked.

British socialist Annie Besant, pictured in 1888: the year that she helped workers at Bryant & May's match factory to win better treatment for themselves.

Japanese writer and feminist Kageyama Hideko, who urged women to unite in their struggle against social oppression. Shortly after this photograph was taken, around 1905, Hideko started a magazine to campaign for women's rights. (Kageyama was her family name; in Japan, surnames are written first. She is also known by her married name, Fukuda.)

Right, US trade union organizer Mother Jones, who led a series of miners' strikes in Pennsylvania in 1900. Here seen in 1917, when she was 87, she lived for another 13 years.

'Bloody Sunday'

'The Guards are coming!' In the dusk of the November evening, the huge, struggling crowd froze for a second. Then, they heard clearly through the mist the clink of harness and the rattle of horses' hooves. Suddenly, the Life Guards appeared in London's Trafalgar Square. They moved into the pack of human bodies, shouldering them right and left, trampling over the weak and injured. Soon, they had broken people up into small groups and the police could now move in with their truncheons.

The crowd turned north, towards the National Gallery. But it was just as bad there. Above the parapet was a dark, jagged hedge: a hedge made of men, and topped with points of shining steel. From the streets at the corners of the gallery, 300 Foot Guards had emerged and now, with bayonets fixed, they dominated the Square. 'Go home — go home.' The demonstration's organizers pushed through the dense, heaving mass of people, hurriedly spreading the message. It would have been madness to go on. And slowly, dragging injured limbs, the men and women went, all 20,000 of them. One hundred and thirty had suffered so badly under the horses' hooves and policemen's truncheons that they had to have hospital treatment. Three later died of their injuries. The police arrested almost 100 more. By six in the evening, 'Bloody Sunday' — Sunday, 13 November, 1887 — was over.

The police, backed by the government, fought to keep Britain's jobless under control and out of sight. This time, though, the thousands thrown out of work by the 'Great Depression' had thought they stood a chance. For London's jobless, meetings in Trafalgar Square had become a way of filling the days and drawing attention to their plight. The traders of London's West End, who feared a drop in visitors from the provinces, and therefore a drop in custom, objected. The police

were called in and started breaking the meetings and processions up. Then all meetings in the Square were banned. But the jobless had friends: many of them middle-class and all of them determined to fight for the right of people to meet and demonstrate in public. They decided to hold peaceful demonstrations Sunday after Sunday in the Square, until the authorities were shamed or bored into withdrawing the ban. Instead, the authorities had called in 4,000 policemen, 300 mounted policemen, 300 mounted soldiers, and 300 soldiers on foot.

All the organizers could do now was publicize the incident, and arrange for the arrested demonstrators to be released on bail. 'A pretty regiment I led out of Millbank Prison, after paying their fines,' remembered socialist Annie Besant, who had led one of the processions to the Square. 'Bruised, clothes torn, hatless, we must have looked a disreputable lot. We stopped and bought hats, to throw an air of respectability over our cortege, and we kept together until I saw the men into train and omnibus, lest with the bitter feelings now roused, conflict should again arise.'

The bitterness and violence would continue, but huge changes were on the way. The poor and unemployed in Great Britain were beginning to resist the oppression of the powerful. In achieving these changes, both Annie Besant and the working class of the 1880s were to play a major part.

Above, 'Bloody Sunday': police and soldiers meet London's unemployed in armed confrontation on 13 November 1887. Here, the police have taken up position round the foot of Nelson's Column in Trafalgar Square.

Left, just outside the Square, police struggle with demonstrators who have walked in procession from Clerkenwell Green. This was the group that included Annie Besant. Her account of the struggle is given in the 'Witness'. Do you think it agrees with what the artist has drawn? Does this mean the artist's picture is accurate? How might the main policeman in the picture have described the fight?

" WITNESS

'The procession I was in started from Clerkenwell Green, and walked with its banner in front, and the chosen speakers, including myself, immediately behind the flag. As we were moving slowly and quietly along one of the narrow streets debouching on Trafalgar Square, wondering whether we should be challenged, there was a sudden charge, and without a word the police were upon us with uplifted truncheons; the banner was struck down, and men and women were falling under a hail of blows. There was no attempt at resistance, the people were too much astounded at the unprepared attack. They scattered, leaving some of their number on the ground too much injured to move, and then made their way in twos and threes to the Square . . . Then ensued a

scene to be remembered; the horse police charged in squadrons at a hand-gallop, rolling men and women over like ninepins, while the foot police struck recklessly with their truncheons, cutting a road through the crowd that closed immediately behind them.'
Source: Annie Besant, in her *Autobiography* (T. Fisher Unwin/Theosophical Society, 1893).

'I have never seen anything like the brutality of the police; the Germans and Austrians, who know what police brutality can be, said the same to me.'
Source: Eleanor Marx, British Socialist.

'Two or three times the mounted men of the police were driven backward by sheer weight of numbers from Charing Cross corner. A mêlée occurred in front of the Grand Hotel, in which two policemen were stabbed and others were struck with stones and sticks. One of the constables who was stabbed was knocked down, kicked about the head, and very dangerously injured. He was taken to Charing Cross hospital on a stretcher. Eventually the mob was overmastered and driven off, leaving half-a-dozen of their number laying on the ground.'
Source: The Daily Telegraph, 14 November, 1887.

"

The dreadful years

For Britain's working class, the 1880s were dreadful years. Workers who were badly paid found they were now even worse off. Huge numbers were thrown out of work at a period when being jobless, and especially being totally without money, was regarded as little better than a crime. They were lost in the abyss of the 'Great Depression'. The Depression's cause was something far beyond the control of any of them. Indeed, it was beyond the control of their employers. Britain, although the pioneer of the Industrial Revolution, was now finding its industries outpaced by rivals abroad, especially by the new industrial giant of the USA. But, as far as their own pockets were concerned, Britain's industrialists had a remedy: by reducing wage bills, they could keep their profits up. As a result, more and more of their workers found themselves facing a future without jobs, without money and without hope.

Dinner-hour for textile workers in the northern industrial town of Wigan. The artist has shown factory workers as the Victorian middle classes liked to think of them in 1874. Try comparing the women's faces with the face of the woman brush-maker, on page 13.

In Victorian Britain, if a family or an individual had no money, they had two basic options. In desperation, they could go to the dreaded workhouse where conditions were made as harsh as possible. Or they could die of want. Many did; The writer Charles Dickens describes the mother of a fatherless family who had not eaten at all for three days. Her husband had already died of starvation. Women's diets, however, were often worse than men's. Men were seen as the breadwinners of the family and so women tended to give them a larger share of food than they had for themselves.

Even if families did have some regular income, life could still be desperately hard. A mammoth survey of London in the late 1880s, Charles Booth's *Life and Labour of the People*, showed that almost a third of the capital's population were living in poverty. Whole families, larger than the one Dickens met, might be living in single-room homes, less than two and a half square metres. They probably shared an outside lavatory with six other families; an outside tap would also be shared. Women struggled desperately to keep their

Sweated labour: helped by one of her children, a woman makes brushes on her kitchen table. Unless she has a husband or older children at work, the tiny amount she earns may be all that her family of eight people has to live on.

families going. If they were married, their husband's wages were too low to be of much help. Women hawked fruit or watercress round streets, worked at home and took in washing. Or they made matchboxes at a few pence a hundred with the children helping.

Matchbox-making was an example of 'sweated labour': work done at home and paid by the amount completed. Another type of sweated labour was garment making. It suited employers, because it kept costs down. For women with families, it was often the only work they could take. For women who could go out to work, some factory jobs were available. These included making the matches with which the boxes were filled. For the tiny wage they earned, the match-makers had to put up with long hours, bullying overseers, and a punitive system of fines for mistakes. The match-makers (men and boys as well as girls and women), were also threatened by the appalling illness of their trade, called 'phossy jaw'. Caused by the phosphorus with which they worked, this decayed the gums, rotted the jaws and could lead to death.

In industrial Britain of the 19th century, there was no compensation for injury caused by inadequate or dangerous working conditions. In order to survive, people had no choice but to take any work that was available.

WITNESS

'The cry of starving children was ever in my ears; the sobs of women poisoned in lead works, exhausted in nail works, driven to prostitution by starvation, made old and haggard by ceaseless work. I saw their misery was the result of an evil system . . . that . . . the worker . . . must remain helpless in the grip of the employing class, and that trade combinations could only mean increased warfare — necessary, indeed, for the time as weapons of defence — but meaning war, not brotherly co-operation for the good of all.'
Source: Annie Besant after visiting London slums; (quoted in *The Life of Annie Besant*, Geoffrey West; Howe, 1929.)

The women walk out

The processions and agitation that led to 'Bloody Sunday' in 1887 had seemed fruitless. But, fruitless though they were, they were symptoms of a steadily deepening anger among the deprived working classes at their treatment by the rest of British society. This anger, linked with determination, would achieve astonishing results.

In July, 1888, the 'match-girls' at the East End factory of Bryant & May walked out on strike. They had been on strike before, against a wage cut and the 'phossy jaw' risk, but without success. This time, to the firm's fury, some of them had told the press about their working conditions. The employers were especially embarrassed by the comparison the press made between the women's wages (between 4s and 13s a week) and the value of the company to shareholders. The year before, £5 shares had been sold for £18. Bryant & May bullied the women to find out who had talked, then sacked four. The rest, all 1,400 of them, walked out, and stayed out.

Socialist and writer Annie Besant had written the press report of the match-workers' plight, so they went to her for help. She and her contacts organized strike pay, whipped up support among London's male workers and the public at large, had questions asked in Parliament, and produced further evidence of the match-workers' desperate working conditions. The women held firm; after a month, the employers gave way, and offered a settlement that Annie Besant said 'far exceeded her expectations'.

If Annie Besant, who had worked like a tiger for the match-girls' success, was surprised, the rest of the world was staggered. The really amazing thing about the women's victory at the time was that it was won by women.

At the Bryant & May match factory in London the women worked at their benches for a 10-hour day in winter, longer in summer. If they left the ground under the bench untidy, they were fined three pence, out of a wage of 48 pence a week.

In Victorian Britain, most women factory workers were employed either in cotton mills, or in the woollen textile trades. The woollen weavers scored an early success for solidarity in 1875, when they went on strike for more pay, and won with the help of the Women's Trade Union League. This picture shows their strike committee.

In the eyes of the average employer, women were that valuable thing: cheap and docile labour. In the eyes of many male workers, they were objects of suspicion. The male-dominated trade unions were mainly concerned with fighting for the family man's wage. Traditionally, women had always been paid lower wages than men. The men feared that their own earning power would be undercut. Many refused to work with women, and frequently excluded them from their unions. Women, it was felt, did not make good fighters for workers' solidarity, or, if they did, it was not suitable work for them. And yet, Annie Besant and the match-workers had succeeded in winning the support of 25,000 of London's male trade unionists, along with the vital contributions they made to the women's strike fund.

After the strike, the Bryant & May workers formed their own large organization, the Union of Women Match-makers with 700 members. The match-workers' success helped stimulate the growth of further women workers' associations all over the country. It also put pressure on male trade unionists to accept women as equals. While only a few unions admitted women in the mid-1880s, many did ten years later. By 1896, the total number of women trade unionists had jumped from under 40,000 to almost 118,000. Many of them were textile workers in Britain's great industrial power base in the North, in the Lancashire cotton mills and West Riding in Yorkshire. But, important though it was, it was not the only great change heralded by the match-workers' strike.

❝❝WITNESS

In 1891, Britain's laundresses joined together in a campaign to get their working conditions protected by law. They worked up to 16 hours a day. Here they are visiting the Home Secretary to explain their demands. Whose side do you think the cartoonist was on: the Home Secretary's or his visitors'?

A TUC delegate at a trade union gathering in 1874: *'The next thing, they'll be wanting to represent themselves.'* **Source:** *Englishwomen's Review,* 1876).

Banding together

In August, 1889, low-paid (and unpaid) Londoners took to the streets again. The docks were on strike: the docks that, almost from the start of London's history, had been the ultimate source of the capital's great wealth. Now, even though trade was picking up again, they stood idle, while 30,000 docks workers paraded their desperate grievances before London's stunned public.

Dock work, at five pence an hour, was not only badly paid; it was also extremely uncertain. When there was any work going, huge crowds would turn up by the dock gates in the hope of being picked for an hour or two's labour. Crushing themselves against the barrier that held them back, men struggled, fought, even died, in their efforts to be seen by the foreman. In order to survive, recalled docker Ben Tillett, they turned themselves into 'mad human rats', who saw in the foreman's glance their only chance of food. In the summer of 1889, the dock employers threatened to cut the low, uncertain wages even further. Led by Tillett, the dockers countered with the demand for a pay rise rather than a cut: for a rate of six pence an hour, or a 'tanner' in Victorian slang. The employers refused: within two days, London's docks were brought to a halt.

Like the match-workers the year before, the dockers had no money to back their strike. The strikers could have been starved back to work. But, again like the match-workers, they used brilliant planning to hold the strike together. They also won support from outside. In Australia, trades union members donated the huge sum of £30,000 towards the dockers' cause. Meanwhile, on their marches through Britain, the dockers carried the main items of their daily diet high above them on poles: dry bread, onions, rotting meat and fish. The public, appalled at the message of these dismal fragments, also poured money into their strike effort. Two years earlier, wealthy Londoners had begged for police protection from the half-starved unemployed. Now, they decided to follow the example of the middle-class thinkers and activists like Annie Besant, who had already pledged themselves to fight poverty. They were ready to give the underpaid their full support in a spirit of solidarity.

In the end, dockers raised £50,000, enough to let them hold out for a month. It was long enough: the unloaded ships, the dockers' marches, and the threat the strike posed to general public order worried both the employers and the government. Negotiations for

Above, Mary Macarthur, general secretary of the recently formed National Federation of Women Workers, inspires a meeting of male strikers in London, in 1908.

Below, scenes from a procession in the 1889 London Dock Strike. Processions like these were hugely successful in arousing public sympathy.

The procession's leader

A country outing for some of Britain's leading socialists: from the left, George Bernard Shaw, Beatrice and Sidney Webb, and Graham Wallas. All belonged to a left wing political group called the Fabian Society, founded in the early 1880s. They campaigned for social reforms through gradual, democratic means. Annie Besant was also a member, and became one of their leading speakers. The middle class Fabians were motivated by a feeling of social solidarity: a sense of duty to every human being, regardless of sex or class.

peace were started, with Britain's Roman Catholic leader, Cardinal Manning, acting as mediator. At last the employers gave the strikers what they had demanded: the docker's tanner. The strikers themselves appointed Ben Tillett as secretary of their own brand-new Dock, Wharf, Riverside and General Labourers' Union. From now on, things would never be the same again for Britain's workers. What the match-workers' walk-out had done for women's trade unionism, the dock strike did for trade unionism as a whole. Workers in many of the other low-paid industries followed the dockers' example and started unions of their own. Union membership soared. The workers at the bottom of the industrial heap were now a force that

employers had to reckon with. By the time the dockers had won their victory, the middle-class groups that had helped to support protests like those in Trafalgar Square were well-established. They aimed to wipe out the injustice they saw all round them. Their members preached the principle of solidarity with other human beings, regardless of class or wealth. In the years after the dock strike, the socialist groups took their principles a stage further and banded together with the 'New Unionism' of the semi-skilled and unskilled workers. The origins of today's Labour Party can be found in their organization.

Dockers on the first float showing how coal was unloaded.

A model of a 'poor docker's baby'.

The match-workers

In mid-sentence, Annie Besant stopped scribbling in her notebook. She looked up and stared at the young factory worker she was interviewing. 'My dear, are you sure you're right?' Annie asked gently.

But the young woman didn't need gentleness. 'Course we're sure — we paid for it, didn't we?' she said. 'Shilling each, that's what we had to give, and that's on top of all the usual cuts: for dirty feet, and talking, and such. And all for a bleeding statue, of Mr bleeding Gladstone . . . ' A friend nudged her elbow, but she went firmly on: ' . . . him so high-minded and all. If they want to be high-minded, why don't they come down here to the factory, and be a bit more high-minded with us? That's what I want to know.' Annie Besant nodded hurriedly, and started to scribble again. 'The cuts; tell me more about that,' she said.

All the young women started talking at once. 'It's the fines . . .' 'They fine us, you see, if we do something wrong . . .' 'Dirty feet, that's threepence,' said the first woman, 'and threepence for talking. And then there's being late — that's one of the worst: for that you lose five pence out of your eight.' 'Eight pence?' repeated Annie Besant.

'Yes, eight pence, that's our daily wage; leastways, that's what a lot of us gets. Four shillings a week, that is, but there's some that get more. My sister gets eight shillings; wish I did, I'm sure.' 'So do we!' chorused the others. 'Four shillings; you must find it hard to manage on four shillings,' Annie Besant said.

'It'd be easier if I got four shillings,' the young woman said grimly, pulling her ragged shawl tighter round her shoulders. 'But I don't, 'cause of the fines, see. None of us ever gets what we should be paid. And I've got my share of my room to pay and all, that's two shillings. And my food . . .'

'Yes, what do you usually eat?' Annie Besant asked. 'Bread and butter; that's what I always have, and tea. Tea's good; it stops you feeling hungry. But . . .' and the young women suddenly grinned, 'then there's my treat. Once a month, I treat myself: I have jam on my bread, and coffee, and everything. It's prime.'

Annie Besant nodded again. She found her throat ached and her lips were shaking. She wanted to weep with rage. As the young women talked on, she scarcely listened. She was used to tales of poverty; she had

Annie Besant, middle class socialist and investigative journalist, shortly before the Bryant & May strike. She was tireless in her efforts to help the casualties of Victorian society; 'I am a socialist,' she once wrote, 'because of the failure of our present civilization.'

seen greater depths of misery than these, often. But to be 16, and have no greater joy in life than a monthly cup of tea or coffee! What a monstrous waste it was. What sort of a future did the young woman have, even if she escaped the jaw disease? To struggle on, marry, have children and then be condemned to yet more struggle, at home, perhaps, drudging over matchboxes until she collapsed every night with exhaustion?

Annie Besant knew that there was one thing that needed to be done immediately: the public had to be told about the misery endured at the match factory. She would write about the match-workers' appalling conditions in words that the public would never forget.

'It's all wrong,' one of them said. 'It's time someone came down here and helped us.' 'Who will help?' Annie Besant asked automatically. But, inside, she knew.

Some of the workers Annie Besant wanted to help: six match-women and one match-boy.

WITNESS

'A typical case is that of a girl of sixteen, a piece-worker; she earns 4s a week, and lives with a sister, employed by the same firm, who "earns good money, as much as 8s or 9s a week."

'Out of the earnings, 2s a week is paid for the rent of one room. The child lives only on bread and butter and tea, alike for breakfast and dinner, but related with dancing eyes that once a month she went to a meal where "you get coffee and bread and butter, and jam and marmalade, and lots of it." '

Source: 'White Slavery in London'; Annie Besant's article on conditions at Bryant & May's, 1888.

'A pretty hubbub we created; we asked for money, and it came pouring in, we registered the girls to receive strike pay, wrote articles, roused the clubs, held public meetings, got Mr Bradlaugh to ask questions in Parliament, stirred up constituencies in which shareholders were members, till the whole country rang with the struggle. Mr Frederick Charrington lent us a hall for registration, Mr Sidney

Webb and others moved the National Liberal Club to action; we led a procession of the girls to the House of Commons, and interviewed, with a deputation of them, Members of Parliament who cross-questioned them. The girls behaved splendidly, stuck together, kept brave and bright all through'.
Source: Annie Besant in her Autobiography (T. Fisher Unwin/Theosophical Pub. Soc., 1893).

In the public eye

Among the men and women of the socialist and trade union movements, Annie Besant cut an unusual figure. She had married a clergyman and, though separated from him, was still his wife. But she was also a self-confessed atheist. She was an educated, middle-class woman of the sort that other women of the time recognized as 'a lady'. But she defied the customs of the day by wearing heavy boots and a workman's red neckerchief, short skirts and a beret perched on top of hair cut unfashionably short. And what she said on subjects ranging from poverty to birth control shocked many women, and many men as well.

In some ways, though, Annie Besant conformed just as closely to what was expected of a Victorian lady as the ones she shocked. The middle-class woman, though barred from many aspects of public life, was permitted and encouraged to do charitable works among the poor. However Annie Besant took her charitable works much further than most. She was not alone either, in her full-hearted championship of people whom many Victorians would have preferred not to know about. Other strong-minded women, like Josephine Butler and Mary Carpenter, had taken up the causes of such out-casts as prostitutes, juvenile (and women) criminals, and many others.

In spite of her atheism, Annie Besant was above all religious by temperament. This was something that the Victorian middle-class encouraged in women. Earlier in life, she had been a devout Christian. During her time as a socialist, the religion into which she poured her emotions and energies was social solidarity. She herself called it a 'crusade for the poor'.

She approached the task with total commitment: 'Deeper and deeper into my innermost nature ate the growing desire to succour, to suffer for, to save. I had long given up my social reputation, I now gave up with ever-increasing surrender ease, comfort, time.' But, however mystical her motives, the results she achieved in her fight against poverty and oppression were real enough. The match-workers' victory, and the spur it gave to unionism, were some of her achieve-ments. The publicity she brought to the Fabian Society was another. (She was thought to be England's greatest orator of the time). Others included the start of a free school meal service for children who needed them. Although her socialist crusade lasted less than five years, the effect she had on British institutions, from schools to Parliament, can still be seen today.

BIOGRAPHY

1847 Born Annie Wood, daughter of a London businessman.
1852 Her father dies; Annie grows up intellectual and deeply religious.
1867 Marries Anglican clergyman Frank Besant; unhappy marriage, later has two children.
1871 Following the severe illness of her daughter, rejects Christianity.
1873 Starts writing: leaves her husband. Radical causes she supports over the next 12 years include equality between the sexes, and birth control.
1883–1888 Owns and edits monthly magazine *Our Corner*.
1885 Becomes a socialist; joins the Fabian society.
1887 Helps to organize protests against wage cuts and unemployment; involved in 'Bloody Sunday'.
1888 Leads matchworkers' strike at Bryant & May.

1889 Embraces Theosophy.
1890 Leaves the Fabian Society.
1893 Visits India, headquarters of the Theosophical Society; decides to live there.
1907 Becomes president of the Theosophical Society.
1916 Becomes president of the Indian Home Rule League, which she founded.
1917 Elected president of the Indian National Congress.
1933 Dies in Madras, aged 86.

'Buy your own string and paste': a matchbox-maker at work in her own home. As Annie Besant recognized, the match-workers' strike harmed people as well as helping them. For the box-makers, lack of work meant starvation.

"WITNESS

What some people said about Annie Besant:
'A mind like a milk-jug'

'I have heard Mrs Besant described as being, like most women, at the mercy of her last male acquaintance for her views on economics.'
Source: Correspondent (male) to the *National Reformer*.

'I have no doubt they have been influenced by the twaddle of Mrs Besant and other socialists.'
Source: Bryant & May director, commenting on the strike.

'The direction of the Fabian Society was done so efficiently by the little group of men already in possession, that Annie Besant must have found, as other women found later on, that as far as what may be called its indoor work was concerned, she was wasting her time . . . She, therefore, became a sort of expeditionary force, always to the front when there was trouble and danger . . . Her powers of continuous work were prodigious. Her displays of personal courage and resolution, as when she would march into a police-court, make her way to the witness-stand, and compel the magistrate to listen to her by sheer force of style and character, were trifles compared to the way in which she worked day and night to pull through the strike of the over-exploited matchgirls.'

Source: Fellow-Fabian George Bernard Shaw, writing in *Dr. Annie Besant: Fifty Years in Public Work* (1924).

///ACTION

1) Weigh the evidence. The Bryant & May women strikers have been labelled as 'match-girls'. Annie called them match-girls herself; it's the name that's still used most often today. Do you think this was an accurate name for them? (Note that the girl described on page 19 was typical.)

2) Using the extracts in the witness on 'Bloody Sunday' on page 11, pick out the words to describe (1) the crowd and (2) the police. Write these words out in three lists, one called *The Daily Telegraph*, the other 'Annie Besant' and the third 'Eleanor Marx'. How do the lists differ? Why do you think this is so? Which writers would be most likely to agree with the other?

Can you rely on one account more than on the other? How can you check the reliability of the accounts?

Banding together for a fair deal: Bryant & May workers, with Annie Besant in the centre, on the strike committee of the Matchworkers' Union they had formed. Do you notice any differences between this picture and the one on page 19? Can you see any faces that are in both pictures?

Daughters, workers, wives

'Help! Help me, please help!' Weak and shaking, the voice came from somewhere down in the ravine. Clinging to each other, the other girls edged to the ravine's brink, and peered over. Their companion was not far below, covered with snow and with her hair undone. Only the bush she was clutching stopped her sliding on down the mountain side to her death. Quickly, following their normal routine, the girls above undid their long sashes, knotted them together, and dangled the make-shift rope over the edge. Then, heaving and scrabbling in the snow with their straw sandals, the helpers took the strain and slowly pulled their friend up. The procession re-formed and set off again: just one group of young factory girls on their way to work in the silk mills of Japan's Suwa region. Towards the end of the last century, scenes like this were common on the Nomugi Pass.

In the 1860s and 1870s, Japan had turned itself from a mainly rural society into an industrial one. By the 1880s, its industries were booming, and the most

successful of all was silk manufacture. Without the money it earned from selling silk abroad, Japan could not have made its lightning transformation into a modern industrial state. But these profits were only obtained by hiring the cheapest possible labour: armies of unmarried girl workers, like the ones on Nomugi Pass. By the 1890s, women formed almost two-thirds of Japan's industrial workforce, and it was their efforts that really propelled Japan into the modern world. But their rewards were tiny.

Conditions in the mills were bad, but there was no shortage of new workers. They were sent there by their parents, often desperately poor farmers, and all their wages went back to their families. To a family on the brink of starvation, the tiny wages unmarried daughters earned could make all the difference between life and death. For the girls themselves, it was enough that they would be fed on rice at the mills, rather than the roots and weeds they ate at home.

Although Japan was trying to become a modern state, many of its social attitudes were still rooted in the past. Its attitude to women was one of the most deeply-rooted of all. Rich or poor, Japanese women were seen as inferior to their menfolk, their fathers and husbands. The supreme goal was always the welfare of the family as a whole. When, for example, a middle-class girl called Kageyama Hideko refused a rich suitor, it was at a price. In return for putting him off, her family would take all the money she was beginning to earn as an assistant teacher. By the standards of the time, it was a fair bargain. Some wealth might have come the family's way from Hideko's rich husband, and now it wouldn't.

At home and at work Japanese girls were expected to be docile, self-denying, ready to accept the restrictions placed on them by tradition. In desperation at their treatment, the workers started to go on strike: Japan's first strike ever, in 1886, was staged by female silk workers. But, even so, male trade unionists despised their efforts. Japanese women seemed as firmly trapped by the demands of a modern industrial state as they had been by those of a rural one. But some of them were already trying to spring the trap.

The foundation of the new Japan's wealth: silk-making in progress. The women silk-makers were regarded as being 'on loan' from their families, rather than workers with their own personal rights.

Above, the woman watches intently as her husband eats. A visitor to Japan, Alice Bacon, reported in 1891 that, from babyhood to old age, a Japanese girl was expected always to depend on her father, her husband or her son.

Below, skilled labour, mass production: decorating pottery by hand in a workshop of the late nineteenth century. How old do you think these workers are? Both Japan and western industrial countries used child labour for many jobs.

〝 WITNESS

'Nomugi Pass is where many factory girls fell down into the ravine. When someone slipped and fell down, we would untie our sashes, tie them together to make a rope, and lower it down to the person in the ravine . . . I can't tell you how many girls died in that ravine . . . we used to tie ourselves to the girls ahead of us so as not to get left behind. Each step of the way we prayed for our lives.'
Source: Survivor of Nomugi Pass, quoted in *Peasants, Rebels and Outcastes*, by Mikiso Hane, Pantheon Books, NY, 1982.

'Women indeed are human beings, but they are of a lower state than men and can never attain to full equality with them.'
Source: Confucius (c. 551 – 479 BC)

'From babyhood to old age, she must expect to be always under the control of one of the stronger sex . . . There is no career or vocation open to her: she must be dependent always upon either father, husband, or son, and her greatest happiness is to be gained, not by cultivation of the intellect, but by the early acquisition of the self-control which is expected of all Japanese women.'
Source: Alice Mabel Bacon, in *Japanese Girls and Women*, Boston, 1891.

'How many unhappy women there must be who marry a man without love because they are unable to be economically independent.'
Source: Kageyama Hideko, in her autobiography *Half My Life*, 1904 (quoted in Sievers, *Flowers in Salt*).

〞

23

'Maidens in boxes'

As Japan's modernization gathered pace, Japanese women began to fight against the way they were treated. But they quickly found that they were on their own. If they needed help and support, it usually had to come from other women. It was just as it had been on Nomugi Pass where the only people who could help the girls cross safely were the girls themselves. They also found that their opponents included traditionalists of both sexes, the government and the police.

Accompanied by her mother, Kishida Toshiko once lady-in-waiting to the Empress herself, began to travel all over Japan. She addressed huge crowds and attacked the idea that women were inferior to men. Thousands of other women travelled to hear Toshiko attack the view that men were better than women because they were stronger. 'If that is true,' she told her delighted audiences, 'why aren't our sumo wrestlers in the government?'

Hideko, still paying off her debt to her family, heard her and found her life transformed. From then on, she too started bringing women together. All the time, the police watched the growth of women's solidarity. At last, at a meeting in Otsu in 1883, they pounced. Toshiko was now daring to attack the kingpin of Japanese society, parental authority. Parents, she told her audience, wrecked their daughters by turning them into 'maidens in boxes'. They restricted them to their traditional role of dutiful and decorative obedience. As a result, Japan's girls were like flowers growing in salt, doomed to wither. Hurriedly, the police stepped in, broke the meeting up, and arrested Toshiko. The former court lady spent eight days in jail.

Two years later, Kageyama Hideko followed her there. She had opened a school for working women, to help make up for the education they had been forced to miss, but the authorities had closed it. Enraged she launched herself into politics, and joined a plot to help the enemies of the Japanese government set up an alternative. The plotters were caught: Hideko's sentence was, not one week, but a year and a half.

During the 1880s, around the time the British matchmakers were beginning to organize, women throughout Japan were uniting in their struggle to be seen as full members of society. They held face-to-face meetings, discussion groups, lectures, and even river picnics which the police could not eavesdrop. But, in 1890, the government came firmly down on the traditionalist

The four main islands of Japan. The silk-making region of Suwa is in central Honshu, to the west of Tokyo.

Sea of Japan

HOKKAIDO

HONSHU

Okaya
Suwa
Tokyo
Kyoto
Otsu
Okayama
Osaka

Pacific Ocean

SHIKOKU

KYUSHU

side. The police were told they could imprison any woman who took part in a political meeting or joined a political group. It was for the police to decide what 'political' meant. Before long, many women were back in their boxes again: isolated from each other and powerless.

Even so, some of them tried to break the isolation down. Political involvement went underground. A few women, including Hideko, joined a socialist group, nicknaming themselves its 'kitchen crew'. From 1905, they went on campaigning for the freedom to be involved in politics, but they had to do it in secret. Meanwhile, many tried to reach their audiences through the written word. They wrote for magazines and newspapers; Hideko herself started a magazine in which she attacked both men and the rich. Both she said, kept women down. Somehow, the message was getting through to women. But the constant threat of fines and prison meant that, on every front, the women's struggle to band together, share ideas and start campaigns was frustrated at every turn. Hideko's magazine was banned, and she and her friends were harried by the police. So were other feminists. As time went on, the cause of women's solidarity seemed more and more hopeless. As Hideko herself once said: 'Beginnings are easy; it's continuing that's difficult.'

Banding together in their fight to take part in political activities, a Tokyo feminist addresses a women's meeting.

Left, Kishida Toshiko: the Imperial lady-in-waiting who was imprisoned for her feminist beliefs. A civilized country, she said, should be ashamed to respect men and yet despise women. Both were needed, to help build the new Japan.

❝❝WITNESS

'Girls marry, and become wives and mothers. Men and women help one another and each carries out various duties: Since the family is the root of the nation, it is the vocation of women who become housewives to be good wives and wise mothers.
Source: Japanese Education Ministry, 1899 (quoted in Sievers, *Flowers in Salt*).

Time of hope?

The crowd cheered, shouted, sang. Another silk worker climbed on the platform and gestured for silence. 'We are not slaves!' she proclaimed. 'We are proud labourers who carry Japan's industries on our shoulders!' In agreement, the crowd shouted again. The year was 1927, and Japan's silk industry, still crucially important, was seeing its biggest strike yet. The main participants were 1,300 women workers, called in by their male colleagues to help shut down a mill at Okaya. The women had joined in without hesitation. Urging other Suwa workers to join them as well, they defended themselves for 18 days against the Suwa mill owners, the police and, most difficult of all, their parents, many of whom were horrified at the way their daughters were defying the employers' authority.

The strike failed in the end, but not before the *Asahi Shimbun*, one of Japan's leading newspapers, had come out firmly against the persecution of the women strikers. The women were now an important part of Japan's industrial muscle. They led marches, they addressed rallies, they had their own section of the Yuaikai, the national workers' association that was playing a key role in fighting for better pay and conditions. World War One was scarcely over before they were rallying all the textile workers in the country to complain to the International Labour Organisation about the way Japan treated its women workers.

Once more, as in the 1880s, they had come out of the boxes in which tradition and their families had placed them. They were banding together in their demands for social justice, just as the match-makers in Britain had done in the 1880s. But the Japanese police were still quick to pounce on women who rocked the political boat. For instance, they beat up a group of women socialists who, in 1921, tried to keep the international labour festival of May Day. Women were still forbidden from joining political parties. However, the economy, far from booming, was now in trouble. Japanese socialists, encouraged by the success of the Russian revolution, were coming into the open. The time was right for all workers to push hard for their demands. The women activists now found they had a new sort of tradition to support them: the one of female self-confidence developed fifty years ago by the early feminists and — in spite of so many difficulties — handed on.

Hideko and the 'kitchen crew', with their demands for women's political and economic freedom, were followed by a new generation of young women intellectuals, who nicknamed themselves the 'Bluestockings'. They demanded emotional and sexual freedom as well. This group merged into another, the New Women's Association, and this continued the long campaign against female seclusion from political life. In 1922, they won the right for women to attend political meetings. This was a small but important victory. Some of their members then started to fight for the vote itself. In 1930, the first-ever national meeting to campaign for the suffrage was attended by 500 women, determined never to be put back in their boxes again. It was, as one of the campaigners said, 'a time of hope.'

Stylishly dressed in western fashions of the 1920s, women demonstrators demand a hearing for their claim for better pay. The speaker, in particular, is full of self-confidence. This is in marked contrast to the women shown on pages 22–23.

Time of hope? Women factory workers march in protest against low wages. How does the picture show that they are now taken seriously by their fellow-workers and the public?

❝ WITNESS

'Many of the issues they raised are still unresolved. But the willingness of Meiji women to make the fight for social change they thought would be beneficial, not only to them, but to their society, has made significant differences in the lives of all Japanese women'.
Source: Sharon L. Sievers, *Flowers in Salt*, Stanford University Press, 1983.

'Our eighteen-day struggle has ended in failure, and we are now forced to accept a temporary truce. We realize more than ever that, in order to improve the miserable conditions in the factory and create a situation in which we can live like decent human beings, we have nothing to depend on but our own efforts.'
Source: Statement by the last 47 Okaya strikers after the strike was broken. (*Peasants, Rebels and Outcastes*, Hane.)

'We are not slaves! We are proud laborers who carry Japan's industries on our shoulders. We must be paid wages in accordance with our contracts. We are not pigs. We must be given food fit for human consumption. Unless our minimal demands are met, we will not retreat even if it means death.'
Source: Woman worker at rally of Okaya strikers, 1927. (*Peasants, Rebels and Outcastes*, Hane).

❞

'Women of the World'

So there they were. Hideko thought she had lost them. Taking the letters out of the drawer, she started to read them again. They came from all sorts of different people, but they ended in much the same way: 'I regret I can no longer subscribe to *Women of the World*'.

The letters from her magazine readers went back to 1907, 21 months ago. Here was one from a Tokyo schoolgirl; someone from her school had been checking up. *Women of the World*, she'd been told, was not proper reading for Japanese girls. Their role was to grow up into 'good wives, wise mothers'. A magazine like this one would give them dangerous thoughts, spoil their chances of a happy life. 'So I am very sorry, but . . .'

Here was a whole bunch, from students training to be teachers. They'd heard that the college authorities were watching their post. Someone had even been snooping round the post office. *Women of the World*, the college said, was a wicked magazine, preaching socialism and subversion. Anyone reading it would be punished. 'We regret, therefore . . .'

And there was another one, from that friend who'd tried to get her neighbours interested. She'd been handing out sample copies to women who lived in her block, and then someone had told the police. 'Hideko, my dear, I know you will understand why I had to stop . . .'

Kageyama Hideko: writer, feminist, ex-convict, magazine founder and housewife. Hideko ran *Women of the World* from home, looking after her three children and her aged mother. As the contents of the magazine showed, she was well aware of the practical side of women's life. Issues included patterns for cutting out kimonos, and advertisements for beauty products.

All together, the letters made a thick bundle. Sighing, Hideko put them down. Unseeingly, she stared at the accounts she'd been doing before she had found them. Had she really done the right thing, after all? It had seemed such a good idea at the time: to start a new magazine, a political magazine for women. Of course, she had planned to have familiar things in it, like sewing hints and recipes. All Japanese women sewed their families' kimonos, cooked their families' rice and fish and bean-curd soup; she did herself. But she wanted the magazine to open up another world for women, to give them a sense of purpose.

It would try to lift the ban that stopped Japanese women going into politics. It would talk about how women were treated, and about what they might do to help themselves. To show what women could do if they tried, the magazine would also have articles on women abroad: fighting women, like Madame Roland in the French Revolution. That was the point of the title: the magazine was meant to help women, by telling them about each other.

But was it really helping? What if those students had been punished, or her friend got into trouble? And that was only a start. The authorities had plenty of ways to bring people into line: prison, for example. Hideko remembered being in prison. It sounded even worse now. Another woman she knew had just spent two months there: her cell had been so tiny you almost bumped your nose if you turned round. Hideko didn't know whether she could bear that. Besides, what would happen to her children if she went to jail again, and her mother? They didn't have much to live on now. Without her, they'd have nothing.

It all came down to the usual thing. Beginnings were easy; it was going on with something that was difficult. Just as she had predicted in that first issue, it really was an endless enterprise. Restlessly, Hideko pulled open the drawer where old copies of the magazine were kept. Yes, there it was: the very first issue of all, the one in which she invited women to rise up and build their own women's movement. Well, some of them were trying. In spite of everything, some subscribers were still there. Hideko rummaged through the pile of bills for the last order form. Yes: in spite of everything, the number they'd had to print last month was nearer 2,000 than it had been. It wasn't a lot, maybe, but *Women of the World* couldn't desert them. Perhaps it could publish safer articles, just for a while, about books, perhaps. Hideko suddenly smiled as she remembered her friends in the socialists' 'kitchen crew'. They weren't meant to be having political meetings, but they were doing it just the same. There were always ways of getting through to other women, if you really tried. Trying was something she was good at.

Come, cast off all footing, for this, at least, we know:
That the Dawn of the day. is coming, and for h the Banners go.

((Morris.))

66 WITNESS

'I used to wake up at five o'clock in the morning and get dressed. When the chief warden came to unlock the ward I sat with the other prisoners and paid respect to her. Then we went to the well to wash our faces and had our breakfast at the working place. After that we started to work . . . some of us sewed red kimonos, some of us wove and spun thread . . . I joined voluntarily with the ordinary women prisoners to finish my assignment every day until two hours before the end of the working time, when I went back to my own ward for reading.'
Source: Kageyama Hideko, *Half My Life*, 1904. (Quoted by Sharlie C. Ushioda in *Fukuda Hideko and the Women's World of Meiji Japan*, Japan in Transition (ed. Conroy and others), Associated University Presses 1984.

'When I look at the conditions currently prevailing in society, I see that as far as women are concerned, virtually everything is coercive and oppressive, making it imperative that we women rise up and forcefully develop our own social movement. This truly is an endless enterprise; we have not reached our goals, but our hope is that this magazine will inspire you to become a champion of this movement.'
Source: Kageyama Hideko, writing in the first issue of *Women of the World*, 1 January 1907. (Quoted in Sievers, *Flowers in Salt*).

Women of the World: **the first page of the first issue. To explain her vision of worldwide female solidarity, Hideko chose a British quotation. It's doubtful whether any British feminist, could have done the reverse!**

KAGEYAMA HIDEKO

In the public eye

Kageyama Hideko was born while Japan was in its last years as a feudal state, in which everyone, men as well as women, were kept firmly in their place by the rules of Japanese culture. By the time she died, Japan was becoming a modern society in more than name. In 1925, all men had been given the vote. Women, struggling under much greater social and legal handicaps, had at least managed to free themselves of the ban on attending political meetings. Very soon, the government would rush into the militarism that would take it into World War Two. It would only be after this that Japanese women would win the right to vote and legally enter public life. But the roots of their success stretched back to the beginnings of the century and

Hideko as a young woman, around the time she was sent to prison for gun-running. To traditionalists, her western-style clothes would have seemed the ultimate in modernity.

beyond: to the point where Hideko and other women started banding together in a fight to be seen as more than the state's ideal of 'good wives, wise mothers'.

Hideko's feminist outlook horrified traditionalists, women as well as men. Their objections ranged from fear that she would undermine society, to distaste for her methods and companions. But what really angered the deeply conservative authorities was the way she mixed feminist beliefs with socialist ones. Women, she said, were oppressed in not one way but two: by men, and by the rich. Their real problem was that they were not themselves allowed to become financially independent: to free themselves from their 'double burden' by being allowed to earn money and keep it. In her ill-fated magazine *Women of the World*, she tried to help them win their freedom. She failed as a magazine proprietor (and in many of her other exploits), but she also preached another message that was more enduring. By her example, women learned that they too could break out of the boxes in which tradition had shut them. She showed them that they could enter public life, and join together to smash what she called the 'corrupt customs of the past'.

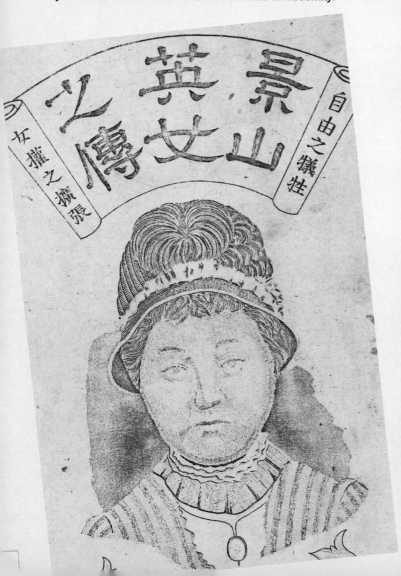

❝ WITNESS

'Japan's Joan of Arc'
Source: Japanese newspaper after the 1885 Osaka incident. (Quoted in Sievers, *Flowers in Salt*).

'A party of women headed by one Ei Kageyama is to come together in Osaka, to deliberate on the subject of Women's Rights. Some of them are said to be of very vulgar origin and others to be of very rude and masculine manners.'
Source: Japanese magazine for women, 1889. (Quoted in Sievers, *Flowers in Salt*).

'I wish to become a woman like Kageyama Hideko.'
Source: Yoshioka Yayoi, who in 1900 founded

Japan's first women's medical school. (Quoted in Sievers, *Flowers in Salt*).

'If this kind of thinking spreads, the disruptive influence it will have upon the family and society in general will be immeasurable. Such thinking bespeaks a deep despair and resentment toward the male sex, feelings born out of a failure to win husbands and settle down as young brides.'
Source: Criticism of a feminist article written by Hideko in 1913. (Quoted in Sievers, *Flowers in Salt*).

❞

◢◢◢◢ACTION BIOGRAPHY

1) Have a discussion. Imagine you are one of the Okaya strikers. Get two friends to be your mother and father. Start a discussion about whether you are right to go on strike. Remember: whatever you say, you have to make it sound respectful! Does this make arguing hard?

2) Weigh the evidence. Read the 'Witness' sections about Nomugi Pass and the Okaya strike again. Can you see anything that is just the same? Why do you think the changes have taken place?

3) Among the letters that Hideko has received is one from a Japanese man criticizing her for publishing *Women of the World*. Write this letter, including as many of the arguments against Hideko as you can think of.

4) Contrast the different views of women's status quoted in the witness on page 23. Then write an article you think Hideko would include in her magazine.

1865 Born Kageyama Hideko in Okayama, in western Japan, daughter of a samurai and a school teacher.
1879 Leaves school; becomes assistant teacher.
1881 Refuses proposal of marriage from rich suitor.
1882 Hears Kishida Toshiko speak on women's rights; as a result, throws herself into working for women.
1883 With her mother, opens a school for girls and women up to the age of 60, to help make up for the basic education they had missed through working.
1884 School closed down by the local authorities. Hideko moves to Tokyo.
1885 The 'Osaka Incident'. In Tokyo, Hideko becomes involved in left-wing politics, joins a group of activists in a plot to set up a liberal government in Korea, becomes an explosives courier. Conspirators, including Hideko, the only woman, arrested and imprisoned in Osaka.
1887 Tried for crimes against the state; sentenced to 18 months in jail.
1889 Released from prison; becomes the partner of fellow-conspirator Oi Kentaro.
1890 Bears Oi's son; leaves Oi the next year.
1892 Marries US-educated liberal Fukuda Yusaku; later they have three children. Becomes a widow in 1900.
1901 Starts another women's school.
1901–1909 Becomes a socialist and works for socialist causes.
1904 Thanks to her autobiography, *Half my Life*, becomes well-known. Starts campaigning against women's exclusion from political activities.
1907 Founds her magazine, *Women of the World (Sekai Fujin)*. Magazine judged subversive; over the next two years, subscribers are frightened off, editors fined and imprisoned, some issues banned.
1909 *Women of the World* forced out of publication by Tokyo court.
1910–27 Continues working for feminist and other social causes.
1927 Dies, aged 62.

Hideko at work. The story she wrote of her life became an instant best-seller. It is still read, and a film has been based on it.

Pittsburgh burns

'Burn them — burn them out!' All over the Pittsburgh railroad yard, men, women and children took up the cry. Twenty thousand people were united in hate: hate for the state National Guards who had been sent in to kill the railroad strike. Instead, they had killed 26 people, children amongst them. That was in the mid-afternoon of 21 July 1877. Now, by mid-evening, the soldiers had taken refuge in the yard's roundhouse. The Pittsburgh crowd wanted to get them out. The strike had started a few days before, in West Virginia. The railroad company that ran the Baltimore and Ohio line announced that workers' wages were to be cut by 10 per cent. The railroadmen were already appallingly poor: they worked 12 hours a day or more, for three dollars a day or less. They lived with their families in shacks by the railway lines. For these, they often had to pay much higher rents to the railroad company than they could afford. To keep their profits level, the companies had already cut their workers' wages several times. The cut of 1877 was the last straw. Starting in the railroad junction of Martinsburg, the strike spread rapidly, winning the support of both the

Right, first shots in the workers' war: the Pittsburgh railroad yard on 21 July, 1877, as the National Guards turn their fire on strikers and the public. The roundhouse, soon to be set alight by the frenzied crowd, is on the right.

Above, US railroad workers take a break. By the 1870s the railroad business was America's biggest industry. Its workers were among the worst treated in the country. A cut in their already low wages sparked off the 1877 strike.

After the fire, little is left of the freight cars except their wheels.

public and of the local troops sent in to regain order. 'The singular part of the disturbance,' commented a Baltimore newspaper, 'is in the very active part taken by the women, who are the wives and mothers of the firemen. They look famished and wild, and declare for starvation rather than have their people work for the reduced wages. Better to starve outright, say they, than to die by slow starvation.' In the yard outside the Pittsburgh roundhouse, freightcars were lined up full of coke and oil. The crowd realized they had their weapons ready and waiting. They set the cars and their

contents on fire; then they trundled them into the roundhouse's walls. The roundhouse caught light and roared into flames. The troops came out at full pelt, pursued by bricks, stones and bullets from the people waiting on the hillside by the tracks.

'It was a wild night,' one of the watchers, a 47-year-old Irish widow called Mary Harris Jones, recalled later. 'The flames lighted the sky and turned to fiery flames the steel bayonettes (sic) of the soldiers.' Over a hundred engines, hundreds of freight cars and 79 buildings were destroyed, and the company was left with a bill for five million dollars. The strikers were only crushed when the US President himself sent troops in to restore order.

The Pittsburgh riot was only one of the waves of fury and despair that broke over the railroad owners' heads in the summer of 1877. The railroad strike that prompted it spread right across the United States of America, and changed American industry for ever. The shots in Pittsburgh and elsewhere by US troops had done more than kill strikers and their supporters. They had ushered in a war between workers and employers which would last well into the next century.

At that time, only six or so national trade unions existed to protect the interests of US workers, much fewer than there had been 10 years before. Although the 1877 strike failed in the end, it showed just what could be achieved if workers started banding together again. The employers, on their side, learned that armed force was needed to bring about victory. Neither side forgot the lesson.

'Solidarity for ever!'

From its start in Pittsburgh and elsewhere, women played an important part in the workers' war. In the coalfields of the east, for example, miners' wives developed a special technique to deal with 'scabs' (workers called in by mining companies to dig coal if the miners went on strike).

The scabs would take mule-carts down the mine with them to bring the coal up in. But, armed with mops, metal dishpans and washtubs, crowds of coalfield women would be waiting for them outside the mine. Then, when the scabs came up from underground, the 'pots and pans raiders' would pour down the hillside towards them — screaming, shouting, banging their dishpans, and putting the mules to flight.

The law usually took the side of the employers. But both employers and law enforcement officers came to

Right across America, workers in trouble had the chance of meeting union organizer Mother Jones. Here, in August 1913, she was leading a strikers' parade in Michigan. By early September, she had gone on to Texas; by the end of it, she had gone on again to Colorado.

Below, the true voice of America? In this poster steel industry bosses are trying to persuade workers back to work by putting the words in the patriotic mouth of 'Uncle Sam'. To make the message clearer, they have printed it in the eight separate languages spoken by their workforce. A high proportion of US workers were immigrants. Because they were so often divided by language and culture, they were difficult to organize in trade unions.

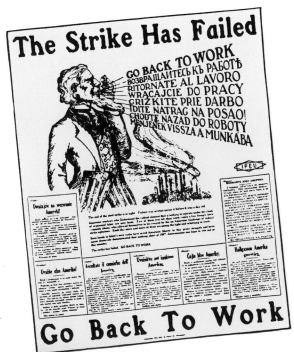

Strikes by women garment workers proved to US trade union officials that women were as determined as men in their union activities. Here, a striker is arrested by the police.

❝ WITNESS

How union organizers were seen:
'These people get near the mines; they appeal to the men daily and hourly in language they understand, and they arouse passions in women and men that already have brought on one fatal collision and produce daily slight encounters.'
Source: *New York Times*, reporting on union organization of Pennsylvania miners' strike, 1900.

'When a Wobbly comes to town, I just knock him over the head with a night stick and throw him in the river. When he comes up he beats it out of town.'
Source: Small-town sheriff in western US quoted in *The I.W.W: A Study of American Syndicalism* by Paul Frederick Brissenden, Columbia University, 1920.

❞

dread the pots and pans raids and their leaders. One dawn raid, at Arnot in Pennsylvania, was led by an Irishwoman in her nightgown, hurriedly bundled up and into action by her husband who was on strike. When the local sheriff told her not to frighten the mules, she gave him short shrift. Another Irishwoman described later what happened: 'She took up the old tin pan and she hit him with it and she hollered, "To hell with you and the mules!" He fell over and dropped into the creek. Then the mules began to rebel against scabbing. They bucked and kicked the scab drivers and started off for the barn.'

This other Irishwoman was Mary Harris Jones, the widow who had watched the roundhouse burn in Pittsburgh in 1877. By now, she was nearly 70. Known everywhere as 'Mother' Jones', she spent her life travelling through the mining areas of America, encouraging miners to join a union and to strike for better pay and treatment. It was Mother Jones who had sent the miners' wives at Arnot careering downhill after the scabs, and led the miners themselves to victory.

The union Mother Jones worked for was the United Mine Workers of America. A young trade union, it was soon to become one of the most powerful protectors of workers' rights in the whole US. By 1905, three-quarters of the country's miners belonged to it. But it was not the only one. Since its low point in the 1870s, American unionism was (in some trades at least)

making a recovery. More and more workers were realizing that they would have to fight hard to win any concessions from their bosses, and that union organization — solidarity — was essential.

The metal workers of the western states now had their own union, too; so did the railway workers; so did the tailors, printers, carpenters, dockers and many others. Most employers, and many other people in authority, hated and feared the unions that forced them to pay workers more. They did all they could to harass union members. But there was something they loathed even more: the 'super-union' set up by the most militant organizations and called the Industrial Workers of the World, or the 'Wobblies'. Its motto was 'Solidarity for ever', and its methods induced not only bitter, long-lasting strikes, but sabotage as well.

The fiery Mother Jones was a founder 'Wobbly', the only woman invited to its founding meeting in 1907. But women all over the States were following her into trade unionism. Taking the militancy of the coalfield wives a stage further, they set up their own trade union league. Male unionists who doubted how well women could fight in the workers' war received a lesson almost as sharp as the one taught the Arnot sheriff: in 1909, 20,000 women garment workers in New York went on strike for more pay, and won. The following year, women in Chicago led many male garment workers into similar action.

The Colorado victims

It was not just in the eastern states of the United States that women showed their solidarity with male workers and with each other. One of their bloodiest battlelines was drawn up in the western state of Colorado. Some of them never left it alive.

Under state law, Colorado miners were in fact given reasonable working conditions. But this law was consistently broken by the employers in the south of the state. In 1913, the United Mine Workers prepared for industrial action to back their demands. 'Rise up and strike', roving organizer Mother Jones told the miners. And on a bitterly cold morning in September, strike they did. Instantly, they were turned out of their homes by mine guards with rifles. With their wives and children, 10,000 miners made their way to colonies of tents the union had set up for them. State troops were

Above, before the massacre, the Ludlow colony had been a large, orderly village of tents, home to about a thousand people. After it had been gunned, set alight, and looted by the troops, little was left. Here, medical workers and a miner's wife search the Ludlow wreckage for survivors.

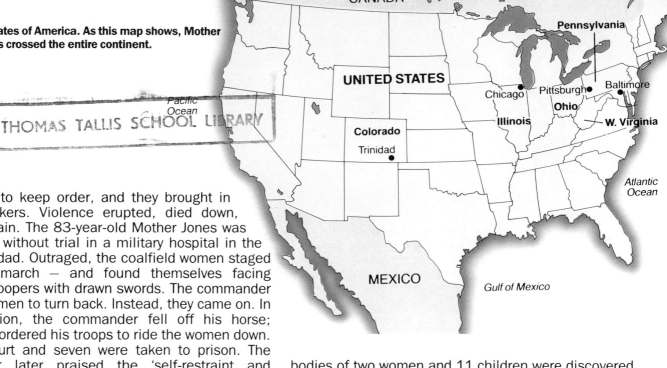

The United States of America. As this map shows, Mother Jones's travels crossed the entire continent.

Pacific
Ocean

CANADA

UNITED STATES

Pennsylvania

Chicago   Pittsburgh   Baltimore

Ohio

Illinois   W. Virginia

Colorado

Trinidad

Atlantic
Ocean

MEXICO   Gulf of Mexico

brought in to keep order, and they brought in strike breakers. Violence erupted, died down, erupted again. The 83-year-old Mother Jones was imprisoned without trial in a military hospital in the city of Trinidad. Outraged, the coalfield women staged a protest march — and found themselves facing mounted troopers with drawn swords. The commander told the women to turn back. Instead, they came on. In the confusion, the commander fell off his horse; furious, he ordered his troops to ride the women down. Six were hurt and seven were taken to prison. The commander later praised the 'self-restraint and patience' of his men.

The guards' treatment of unarmed women was an important propaganda victory for the miners, though it was victory at a price. Very much worse was to come, however, and this time the price was death. On 20 April 1914, fresh trouble flared at the big tent colony of Ludlow. A small scale clash suddenly turned into a shoot-out between troops and miners that lasted a day. Some of the miners' wives and children hid in pits dug under the tents. Later, the victorious troops turned their machine-guns on the empty tents, looted them, and set fire to the wreckage. The next day, the dead

bodies of two women and 11 children were discovered under a tent floor. The 'Ludlow Massacre' transformed the course of the strike. It became an armed rebellion in which 50 people died; it almost grew into a nation-wide rising. Mother Jones travelled from state to state, describing the horrors to which the strikers had been subjected. She even lobbied President Woodrow Wilson, who was called in to help make peace. In the end, peace of a sort was made. The employers agreed to let miners bargain for better pay and conditions, but not through the union. The union, Mother Jones said later, lost in Colorado because it had only the US Constitution behind it. 'The other side had bayonets. In the end, bayonets always win.'

Below, Ludlow, 1914: the troops move in. The Ludlow massacre was triggered off by both guards and strikers believing that the other side was about to attack. It is still unclear which, if either, of them was right.

" WITNESS

'Woman carrying American flag knocked down with butt of gun and flag torn from her hands by militia men. Cavalry slashed another woman with a sabre, almost severing an ear from her head. Militia men jab sabres and bayonets into backs of women with babes in their arms and trample them under the feet of their horses. Mothers with infants thrown into military prison. Feeling is intense. Union officers doing everything to pacify the people.'
Source: Union official John Lawson, in cable to the United Mine Workers 1914 convention, describing

Trinidad Women's march. (Quoted in *Mother Jones: The Miners' Angel* by Dale Fetherling; So. Illinois University Press, 1974).

'The soldiers . . . set fire to the tents of Ludlow with oil-soaked torches . . . After it was over, the wretched people crept back to bury their dead. In a dug-out under a burned tent, the charred bodies of eleven little children and two women were found — unrecognizable.'
Source: Mary Harris Jones, describing the Ludlow Massacre in her *Autobiography* (see page 39).

"

On the march

Mother Jones was furious. Right through the anthracite mines of eastern Pennsylvania, men were joining the union and coming out on strike. They were coming out by the thousand in Scranton and Shamokin and Valley Battle. But in Coaldale in the Panther Creek the men were still at work. They were betraying their comrades in the workers' war; they were betraying themselves. All they needed was a leader; well, Mother Jones would give them one. She'd give them several; then they wouldn't go crawling to the mine-owners any more.

In nearby McAdoo, everyone knew the black-clad figure with her lace collar and the bonnet with pansies on it. 'Mother Jones is back', they said as she bustled down the street. 'How're you doing, Mother?' 'Want any help, Mother?'

'That's right, boys,' said Mother Jones. 'But it's not you I want. I want my army.' There was a laugh, and the crowd moved and rippled as the women in it pushed forward. 'Do we take our dishpans?' shouted one of them. 'That's right,' said Mother Jones again. 'We're off to Coaldale, tonight.'

Mother Jones, aged 87 in 1917. She was still campaigning when she died 13 years later.

Right, 'Pots and pans raids' were not a speciality of Pennsylvania. Here, a scab gets the same treatment from miners' wives in Ohio. Similar techniques of demonstrating social disapproval were also employed right across the world, from Britain to Australia.

Left, family life in a miner's camp. Mother Jones is helping a miner's wife with her children. No-one knows exactly how the elderly union organizer got her nickname, but scenes like this made sure that it stuck.

'What about our kids?' another woman called. 'Get your men to look after your kids,' Mother Jones replied.

'But what about you, Mother? Coaldale — that's fifteen miles, over the mountains. That's a long way, by night.'

Mother Jones drew herself up. 'Now, you just listen to me,' she said. 'I may be 70, but that don't mean a thing. That don't mean I can't go with you and raise hell up in the mountains. I'm a hellraiser — and, please God, I'll go on being a hellraiser till the day I die.'

Slowly, the march wound over the mountain in the dark. If noise could have been turned into light, it would have been as bright as day. The women clashed and smashed their metal dishpans together. A band played. The great crowd of miners who had followed the women cheered. Waiting on the road to the mine, the soldiers hired by the mining firm heard the racket, and fixed their bayonets. In the dawn light, they could see a huge band of people bearing down on them. 2,000, 3,000, even five . . . who knew? At the front walked a dumpy, cosy-looking figure in black, like somebody's grandmother. They all came closer and closer.

'Halt! Move back!' cried the troop commander. But, at the head of her army, the little old grandmother came steadily on. She came up to the ranks of fixed bayonets and looked the commander in the eye. 'I'll charge bayonets,' he warned. But she ignored him. 'Colonel,' she said, 'the working men of America will not halt nor will they go back. The working man is going forward!'

WITNESS

Mother Jones takes up the tale of what happened at Coaldale and describes what she told the Commander:

' "I'll charge bayonets," said the Commander.
'On whom?'
'On your people.'
'We are not enemies,' said I. 'We are just a band of working women whose brothers and husbands are in a battle for bread. We want our brothers in Coaldale to join us in our fight. We are here on the mountain road for our children's sake, for the nation's sake. We are not going to hurt anyone and surely you are not going to hurt us.'

'They kept us there till day-break and when they saw the army of women in kitchen aprons, with dishpans and mops, they laughed and let us pass. An army of strong mining women makes a wonderfully spectacular picture.'

'Well, when the miners in the Coaldale camp started to go to work they were met by the McAdoo women who were beating on their pans and shouting "Join the union! Join the union!" '

'They joined, every last man of them, and we got so enthusiastic that we organized the street car men who promised to haul no scabs for the coal companies. As there were no other groups to organize we marched over the mountains home, beating on our pans and singing patriotic songs.'

Source: *Autobiography of Mother Jones*, by Mary Harris Jones (ed. by Mary Field Parton, introduction by Clarence Darrow; pub. Charles H. Kerr, Chicago, 1925; reprinted by Arno Press, New York, 1969).

MARY H. JONES

In the public eye

Hell-raiser and sweet old lady, miners' angel and old hag: these are just some of the names that attached themselves to American labour organizer Mary Harris Jones. In the cause of promoting solidarity with union workers across the United States, she was afraid of nothing and no-one. She even took on the US President. Those she supported adored her, even while she scolded them; the nickname 'Mother' said it all. Those she fought came to dread her appearance on the picket lines.

Where did her power lie? It was not in a reputation for lasting achievement, since she had none. Often, the strikes she helped to organize failed. When they succeeded, her strong words and uncompromising approach were frequently an embarrassment to the negotiators. She had little money and no grand connections. What she did have, though, was an outstanding skill for public relations, for publicizing her cause, winning support for a strike, cheering faint-hearts and shaming backsliders into mending their ways. For shock tactics, she often drew on traditions already established among the coalfield women for expressing their anger and hate. For protection, she could to a large extent rely on the reverence her image of the 'sweet old lady' exacted, even among the most aggressive. As shown in Colorado, this protection was something that her younger female supporters could not count on. The women, however, shared something of her power. This power was drawn from the way American society fitted them into their traditional roles of wives and mothers. Abuse of these dependent beings could, and did, fan public unease into public fury. The main difference between Mother Jones and the Ludlow victims was that she survived all threats, and they did not.

Mother Jones on the march. One of the secrets of her success was her extraordinary physical energy. By this time, she was in her late 70s at least.

❝ WITNESS

'Your honour, there is the most dangerous woman in the country today.'
Source: Prosecuting attorney at Mother Jones' trial for contempt of court, West Virginia, 1902 (from Mother Jones' Autobiography).

'It seems to me that it would have been better by far for her to follow the lines and paths which the Allwise Being intended her sex to pursue. There are many charities in life which are open to her in which she could contribute largely to mankind in distress, as well as avocations and pursuits that she could engage in of a lawful character that would be more in keeping with what we have been taught and what experience has shown to be the true sphere of womanhood.'

Source: Federal Judge John J. Jackson, speaking at the West Virginia trial. (Mother Jones: the Miners' Angel, Fetherling.)

'She was a sweet old lady. I remember when she came here seven years ago. I knew she was a scrapper and I expected to see a tough old person with a hard voice. Instead, I saw an old-fashioned woman, kind of like the old ladies in the movies that sit at home and do embroidery. You couldn't have helped loving her.'
Source: Young miner after Mother Jones' death, 1930 (quoted in Mother Jones: the Miners' Angel, Fetherling).

❞

As winter grips Denver, Colorado in 1913, Mother Jones leads a miners' procession to protest against the state's use of troops in the coalfield. The protest was unsuccessful. Later, Mother Jones was imprisoned, and the Ludlow victims were killed.

BIOGRAPHY

1830 Born Mary Harris in Cork, Ireland.
1835 Mary's father emigrates to USA, followed by his family; later, they move to Canada. On leaving school, Mary becomes a teacher, later on a dressmaker.
1861 Mary marries ironworker George Jones in Memphis, USA; later, they have four children.
1867 Husband and children die in yellow fever epidemic. Mary starts work again as a dressmaker, in Chicago.
1871 Loses all possessions in great Fire of Chicago; joins the Knights of Labor, a secret workers' organization.

1877 Involved in Pittsburgh railroad strike.
1880s Involvement in labour organization and agitation grows.
1890s Becomes labour organizer for the United Mine Workers of America.
1900 Leads victorious strike at Arnot, later at other Pennsylvania mines; wins widespread fame for her use of the 'pots and pans raid' technique for intimidating blacklegs.
1902–1910 Involved in coal miners' strikes in West Virginia and Colorado; involved with copper mines' strikes in Arizona.
1911 Returns to help West Virginia miners: sentenced to 20 years' imprisonment

by military court; freed by state governor.
1913–1914 Goes back to Colorado to organize renewed strikes; arrested three times; publicizes Ludlow Massacre.
1915–1919 Supports New York garment workers and streetcar workers in their strike action; later the 1919 steel strike.
1930 1 May: celebrates her hundredth birthday.
1930 30 November: dies.

◢◢◢ ACTION

Here is an account written by a journalist who was on the McAdoo march: *'Within sight of the collieries the marchers had come all the distance to close, the front ranks of the strikers were met by the bayonets of the Pennsylvania National Guard. The weary miners turned back without accomplishing the purpose of its midnight march.'* Quoted in: *Mother Jones: the Miner's Angel*, Fetherling.

In what ways does this report differ from Mother Jones' description? Can you explain why they differ? Do you think differently about Mother Jones' writings?

41

Conclusion

In Great Britain during the 1880s, Annie Besant tried to fight poverty. In Japan, Kageyama Hideko embarked on a campaign against the oppression of women that would last well into the twentieth century. In the United States, Mary H. Jones started to take on employers, the police and the military in her long-running battle for better pay and working conditions for trade unionist miners. Although their struggles took place in different countries and against different enemies, all three used much the same weapons.

If solidarity is about bringing people together, what do you think would be an effective way to appeal to people's feelings? The most important weapon the three women had was the written, or spoken, word. Hideko was a gifted writer, and Annie Besant was a good one; both founded magazines, and put their communication skills at the service of the causes they were fighting. In addition, Annie Besant was a brilliant public speaker, so was Mary H. Jones.

Another thing that helped all three was their personal life, or, rather, the lack of it. Annie Besant was separated from her husband. Mary H. Jones was a widow. Hideko was famous for her emotional entanglements, but she was still much more free than the average Japanese woman. The three campaigners were therefore at liberty to travel, to lead their own lives, and to take on heavy commitments outside the home; all activities that might well have been strongly discouraged by a husband or a husband's family.

How far do you think they all succeed in inspiring a sense of solidarity in others? Of the three, Annie Besant's achievements were the most obvious: the victory over Bryant & May's, the formation of the match-workers' union, the boost her public speaking gifts gave to the Fabians. Mary H. Jones's successes, lasting only days or even hours, were far less permanent. All the same, the difference she made to her hearers' feelings about themselves probably lasted much longer. The same is true of Hideko who, on the surface, failed at everything she did. Her great achievement, though, was that she tried, and that she inspired women who came later.

Evidence for this sort of success is often hard to find. Until recently, women's activities attracted much less notice than men's. But the fact that this evidence has so far remained invisible does not make the women's achievements any less important.

BOOKS TO READ

GREAT BRITAIN
Essential reading, for both young people and adults: **The Match Girls' Strike 1888**, by Reg Beer (Labour Museum Pamphlets Number Two); available from the National Museum of Labour History, 20 Grange Thorpe Drive, Burnage, Manchester M19 2LG.

Very useful: **Annie Besant — An Autobiography**, by Annie Besant; published by T. Fisher Unwin, 1893.
Annie Besant, by Rosemary Dinnage, published by Penguin, 1987.

For further information, try to visit the National Museum of Labour History (this also publishes the strike register of the Bryant & May workers); also the Fawcett Library at the City of London Polytechnic, Old Castle Street, London E1.

JAPAN
Essential reading: **Flowers in Salt: The Beginnings of Feminist Consciousness in Modern Japan**, by Sharon L. Sievers; published by Stanford University Press, California, USA, 1983. A major English-language source on Kageyama Hideko, her feminist colleagues, and the social background against which they operated. Don't be put off by the title; the text is aimed at adults, but it is clear and highly readable. (Remember that books often refer to Hideko by her married surname, Fukuda.)

The **Japan** volume in the **Time-Life 'Library of Nations'** series is excellent. For younger readers, there is also **Big Business . . . in Japan**, by Anna Sproule, published by Macdonald Educational, 1986.

For help with further information, contact the Japan Information Centre, 9 Grosvenor Square, London W1.

USA
Essential reading: **Mother Jones — The Miners' Angel**, by Dale Fetherling; published by Southern Illinois University Press, USA, 1974. Again aimed at adults, but very clear.

Also useful: **The Autobiography of Mother Jones**, edited by Mary Field Parton, foreword by Clarence Darrow; first published by Charles H. Kerr, Chicago, USA, 1925. Two re-published editions available, both American; can be ordered through the British library system and the Fawcett Library. (It's important to remember that Mother Jones was very old when she composed this — and she often got her facts muddled up!)

Mother Jones: The Most Dangerous Woman in America by Linda Atkinson; published by Crown, New York, USA, 1978. (Not available in Britain.)
For all matters of American history, the library maintained by the United States Information Service is invaluable. The USIS is part of the US Embassy, at 24 Grosvenor Square, London W1. ESSENTIAL to make an appointment.

▰▰▰ACTION▰

Below is the banner of Britain's National Federation of Women Workers, of which Mary Macarthur (shown on page 16) was president, then secretary. As is proved by the reverence paid to national flags, banners and emblems have an important role to play in promoting **solidarity**; so do their close relations, posters and advertisements. Without these, a movement has problems in winning people to the cause at all.

Designing an effective banner or poster is an art. See if you have the talent for it by designing something for the three main campaigns described in this book.

For instance, you could design a banner for the

Matchmakers' Union, an advertisement for *Women of the World (Sekai Fujin)* and a 'join the union' poster for Mother Jones to use. You'll find it helps if you work out exactly what you're aiming your design to do.

Do you want to give people facts? Do you want to influence their feelings? Do you want them to take some immediate action, or to go away and think?

What do you think Annie Besant, Hideko or Mother Jones would have wanted to achieve?

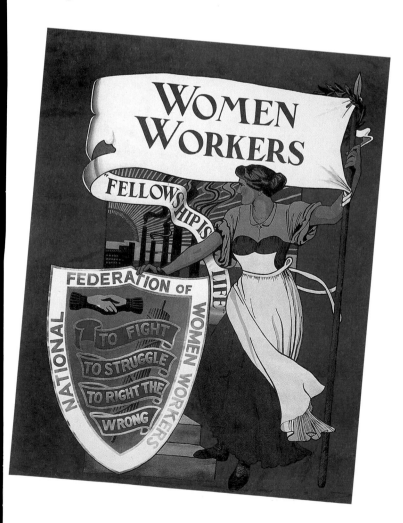

Time chart

1792: Britain ✳ 1789 Outbreak of French Revolution
Former governess **Mary Wollstonecraft** publishes her *Vindication of the Rights of Women*, in which she demands equal rights for the 'subject race'.

1793: France
Manon Roland, revolutionary, dies under the guillotine, executed by rival faction in the French Revolution. Solidarity, or 'fraternity', was one of the Revolution's main watchwords.

1844: USA ✳ 1815 Napoleon's defeat at Waterloo
Sarah G. Bagley, cotton worker, successfully organizes female textile workers in New England into a female trade union.

1868: Britain ✳ 1861–1865 American Civil War
Millicent Garrett Fawcett, suffragist, makes her first public speech on votes for women.

1874: Britain ✳ 1868 Meiji Restoration; Japan
Emma Paterson, former bookbinder's apprentice, founds the Women's Protective and Provident League (re-organized as Women's Trade Union League in 1891).

1883: Japan
Kishida Toshiko, feminist, makes her 'Maidens in boxes' speech. ✳ 1877 National Railroad Strike, USA
✳ 1886 Women Silk Workers' Strike, Japan

1888: Britain ✳ 1887 'Bloody Sunday', London
Annie Besant, middle-class socialist, leads the matchworkers' strike at Bryant & May's London works.

1898: Russia ✳ 1889 London Dock Strike
Alexandra Kollontai, aristocrat and future revolutionary, rejects her wealthy background to devote herself to the workers' cause.

1903: Britain
Emmeline Pankhurst, suffragette, founds the Women's Social and Political Union.

1904: China/Japan
Jiu Jin, Chinese revolutionary, founds, (in Japan) a women's association for Chinese feminists and women patriots.

1907: Japan
Kageyama Hideko, feminist and socialist, founds her magazine, *Women of the World*.

1910: USA
Bessie A. Hillman, founder of the Amalgamated Clothing Workers of America, helps lead five-month strike of women and men in Chicago's clothing industry.

1914: Germany ✳ 1914–18 World War I
Rosa Luxemburg, revolutionary and feminist, on the out-break of world war I, founds the pacifist Spartacus League.

Glossary

Class Social rank. The main class divisions are upper, middle and working class. Class divisions were (and are) thought of as particularly important in Great Britain, but they exist in other cultures as well.

Demonstrate/Demonstration When people want to demonstrate their feelings, they show them openly. Demonstrations about an issue of public importance involve the public expression of feeling by meetings, marches and so on. A demonstration can be either for or against an issue; the right to hold a peaceful demonstration is an important one in any society that claims to uphold individual freedom.

Feminism Social and political movement aiming to give women the right to define their place in society generally, at work and before the law.

Feudal system A system of running society in which land-owning groups hold power. The Japanese feudal system was slightly different from the European one of the Middle Ages. The Japanese system lasted until the 19th century.

'Great Depression' In the 1870s and 1880s, both British agriculture and British Industry hit hard times. Competition from other countries was damaging British trade; jobs were lost as a result, and wages fell. This period is often called the 'Great Depression'; it should not be confused with the other Depression that caused huge unemployment in Britain in the 1930s.

Industrial/Industrialists The word 'industrial' has several related meanings. An 'industrial' town is one where the main source of income is work in a heavy or traditional industry, such as steel-making or textiles. An 'industrialist' is someone who makes money out of an industry, not by working in it, but by owning it. 'Industrial' issues or problems are usually connected, not with industrialists, but with the workforce. In the USA, these may be called 'labor issues'.

'Industrial Revolution' The major change, pioneered by Britain, that took place in the technology of manufacturing in the late 18th century and early 19th century. During the Industrial Revolution muscle power was replaced by steam or water power. The use of machines meant a change in place of work from home to factory. Women and men's jobs changed as a result.

Labor US spelling of 'labour'; labour/labor history, issues, problems etc all focus on those who work in industry. Trade unionism is a labour issue.

Militarism A readiness to adopt the aims and ideals of the military as the guiding spirit in social or political life. Japanese militarism in the 1930s led Japan into the Second World War.

Negotiation The process of reaching agreement through bargaining. An important part of the final stage of a campaign on pay or any other issue.

'New Unions' The unions set up for, and by, British unskilled workers as a result of the industrial struggles of the late 1880s. The Matchmakers' Union was one, and so was the Dockers' Union.

Pay claim In labour language pay claims are demands for higher wages. They are often expressed in percentages: a 10 per cent claim is a demand for a wage rise that equals a tenth of what the worker is getting already.

'Phossy jaw' Workers' name for phosphorus necrosis, a disease caused by inhaling phosphorus fumes. In Victorian Britain, about two-thirds of the workers in an average match factory risked getting it.

Propaganda Information that is directly favourable to the propagandist's cause, or directly unfavourable to that of any opponents. It may or may not be true.

Reforms Changes that produce improvements demanded by the reformers.

Sabotage The deliberate damaging of, usually, industrial or military equipment and property.

'Scabs' Strike-breakers. When a business is hit by a strike, the employer can try to keep production going by bringing in workers who are not members of the union organizing the strike. They are therefore not bound by its strike call. An outstanding cause of labour friction.

Shares To help businesses run, money is raised by selling 'shares' in themselves. Everyone who buys a share becomes a part-owner of the business, and will get some of the business's profits. These part-owners are called 'share-holders'. Shares can be bought and sold. If a business is doing very well (as Bryant & May was just before the strike) share-holders can sell their shares for a lot more than they paid for them. This is good business for the share-holders, but none of this extra wealth goes to the people who really made it: the workers.

Socialism A system of organizing a country in which the whole population owns the businesses and other things that create the country's wealth. Industries would be owned, not by industrialists and share-holders eager to improve their profits, but by the State. It would be up to the State to ensure that the wealth was distributed fairly to everyone.

Solidarity Unity of purpose between individuals or groups. The word 'solid' can also be used in this sense. It means that someone is totally committed to the views or intentions being discussed.

Strike Refusal to work. Usually, this refusal is planned in advance, but can also be spontaneous. A key weapon in labour disputes.

Trade Union Workers' organization formed to protect their interests: especially pay and working conditions.

United States Constitution The set of written rules that govern the way the USA is run.

Index